LOOK WHAT MOUTHS CAN DO

LOOK What ANIMALS Can Do

LOOK WHAT MOUTHS CAN DO

CAN DO

LOOK What ANIMALS Can Do

BY D. M. SOUZA

Lerner Publications Company · Minneapolis

photo on page 2: **A giant anteater hunts for insects using its long snout.**

Lerner Publications Company
A division of Lerner Publishing Group
241 First Avenue North
Minneapolis, MN 55401 U.S.A.

Website address: www.lernerbooks.com

Library of Congress Cataloging-in-Publication Data

Souza, D. M. (Dorothy M.)
    Look what mouths can do / by D. M. Souza.
      p.   cm. — (Look what animals can do)
    Includes bibliographical references and index.
    ISBN-13: 978–0–7613–9462–4 (lib. bdg. : alk. paper)
    ISBN-10: 0–7613–9462–1 (lib. bdg. : alk. paper)
    1. Mouth—Juvenile literataure. I. Title. II. Series: Souza, D. M. (Dorothy M.) Look what animals can do.
  QL857.S68 2007
  573.9'95—dc22   2005032481

Manufactured in the United States of America
1 2 3 4 5 6 – DP – 12 11 10 09 08 07

TABLE OF CONTENTS

LOOK AROUND.
MOUTHS ARE EVERYWHERE.

A young girl is biting into a juicy apple. Several birds are cracking sunflower seeds at a feeder. A mosquito is sucking blood from a boy's arm.

But mouths are doing more than eating and drinking. With lips, tongues, teeth, or jaws, some animals are yawning, spitting, chattering, and whistling. And they can do so much more.

The great white shark has a huge mouth with sharp teeth. Its teeth are shaped perfectly for what it eats.

Tigers, for example, use their teeth to catch and kill **prey**, the animals they eat. Prairie dogs greet one another by touching lips. Cats use their tongues to clean their fur.

Other animals sometimes use their mouths as nurseries. A few often turn them into buses to carry around their young. Others use them as hiding places for weapons. You may be surprised when you discover what mouths can do.

A tiger's teeth are many different sizes. The biggest ones, called canines, are used for killing prey.

TRICKY HUNTER

An archerfish is hunting in a grassy swamp in India. It has eaten every insect floating or swimming in the water. But it is still hungry.

The fish swims closer to the surface to search for more food. From above, it does not even look like a fish. Its body is narrow like a knife. Black and white markings on its back make it look like the leaves around it.

The archerfish spots a spider hanging from a branch above the water. The archerfish pokes the tip of its mouth upward and lowers its tail. It now looks as if it is standing in the water.

The archerfish sees its prey and gets ready to strike.

Next, the fish presses its tongue against the roof of its mouth and spits. A jet of water shoots straight up and hits the spider. The creature falls into the fish's open mouth.

In a few minutes, the archerfish spots an insect flying high above the water. This time, it does not spit but jumps out of the water. In a flash, it leaps into the air and gulps down the flier. No bug is safe near this tricky fish's mouth.

The archerfish shoots an insect with a spray of water from its mouth.

BIG MOUTH

The day is warm, and twelve hippos are cooling themselves in a lake in East Africa. A big **bull**, or male, yawns as he stands guard. His mouth is one of the largest in the animal kingdom.

The hippo's two big lower teeth are almost as long as your arm. They are sharp and pointed and can kill a small animal in one bite. When the hippo closes his mouth, these long teeth fit into two pockets in his upper jaw.

Another male hippo enters the water from the opposite shore. He is not wanted here. The big bull moves toward the newcomer with his mouth open. The stranger also opens his mouth and shows his long, curved teeth.

Male hippopotamuses open their mouths wide to show they are ready to fight.

The big bull rushes toward the stranger. He dives underwater, fills his mouth with water, and throws it on the other hippo. The stranger dives and does the same thing.

For almost an hour, the two hippos fight. Soon the stranger's flesh is bleeding. He is no match for the big bull. The stranger lowers his head and moves back onto land. For a long time, he will carry the teeth marks of the big bull on his flesh.

The hippopotamuses fight by throwing water with their mouths. They also bite with their long teeth.

PAPER MAKERS

A black and yellow insect lands on a fence. The insect is a paper wasp queen. She has spent the winter resting in a woodpile. Now she is ready to build a nest.

The queen bites off a small sliver of wood from the fence. She chews and mixes the wood with a liquid in her mouth called **saliva**. Then the queen flies to a nearby shed.

The queen lands under the overhanging roof. The sliver of wood in her mouth is now a tiny wad of paperlike material. Carefully the wasp spits out the wad and presses it against the underside of the roof.

A paper wasp begins building its nest. It spits out paperlike material from its mouth.

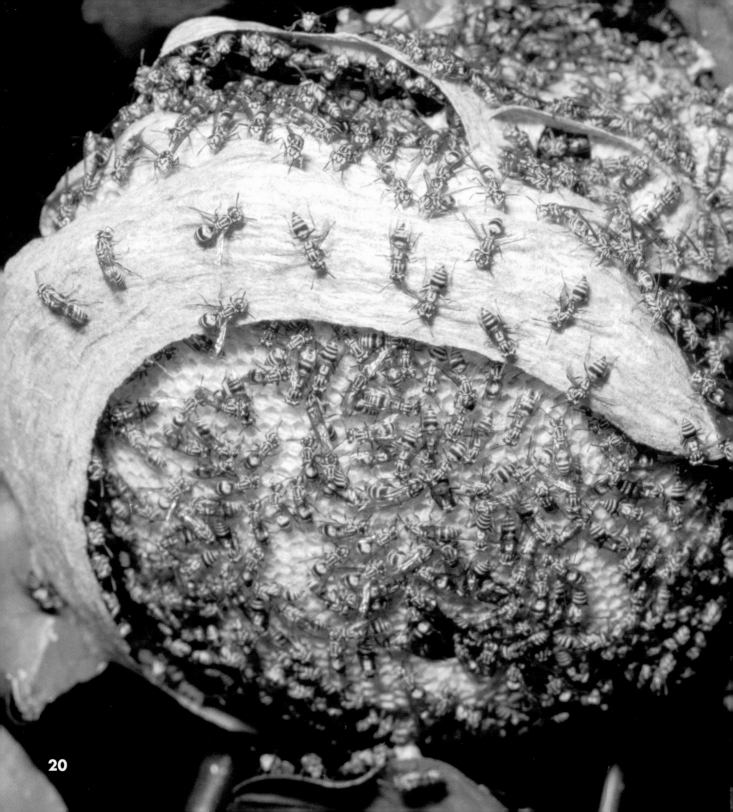

Again and again, the wasp flies between the fence and the shed. Again and again, she chews bits of wood and spits them out in wads. Other paper wasps arrive to help chew, spit, and build the nest.

Soon the nest is full of tiny **cells**, or rooms. The cells are side by side with openings facing downward. The whole nest looks like an open umbrella dangling from the roof's overhang.

The nest is finished. The queen lays one egg in each cell. Other wasps stand guard until the eggs hatch. Each day, the humming sounds of young wasps grow louder. Before long, their mouths will be turning slivers of wood into more paper nests.

Paper wasps guard the nest until young wasps are ready to fly away.

BUS RIDES

A female alligator is swimming in a Florida swamp. As she swims, she keeps an eye on something nearby. Not far from the water's edge is a nest piled high with leaves and twigs.

The female has been guarding the nest for more than two months. Forty eggs with growing baby gators are hidden inside. The eggs are almost ready to hatch.

One day the female hears soft grunts and barks coming from the nest. She crawls onto the land. Using her mouth, she sweeps away some of the mud and grass on top of the nest. Several baby gators have already broken out of their shells.

These baby alligators have just hatched from their eggs.

Carefully the female alligator scoops up the young with her mouth. She holds them on her tongue. Then she heads toward the water.

When the alligator reaches the water, she opens her mouth. She shakes her head gently, and the baby gators slip out. They begin swimming and playing in the water.

Again, the female returns to her nest to see if more of her young have hatched. Some babies find their way to the water by themselves. But others ride in their mother's tooth-filled mouth. It is the best and safest bus ride they will ever take.

A baby alligator takes a ride in its mother's mouth.

POWERFUL SALIVA

A boy holds the side of his head. He feels weak and frightened. A neighbor's dog has almost bitten off his ear. One of his parents rushes the boy to the hospital. Doctors work quickly to try to sew his ear back in place. After many hours, they succeed.

But days later, blood stops flowing through the ear. The boy is in danger of losing his ear. The doctors decide to use leeches.

Leeches are wormlike creatures that live around the world in ponds, lakes, and rivers. Some leeches are so small they could fit on the tip of your fingernail. Others are longer than a ruler. Most drink blood they suck from insects, fish, frogs, turtles, and animals called **mammals**.

The leech's mouthparts can be seen at the top of this photo.

Doctors sometimes use specially raised leeches to treat bruises or black eyes. A fall or a blow to the body can cause blood to collect under the skin. Doctors place leeches on the injured area. The leeches draw out the pooled blood.

Doctors also use leeches after surgeries to help body parts heal. Two leeches are placed on the boy's ear. With their sharp teeth, the animals make small Y-shaped cuts in the skin. The leeches begin their blood feast. The boy does not feel anything because the leeches' saliva deadens the pain. The saliva also contains a chemical that keeps blood flowing.

The blood starts flowing through the boy's ear. In a few days, the boy is feeling better. Soon he is able to leave the hospital. Leeches and their powerful saliva have helped save his ear.

A leech uses its teeth to make small cuts in the skin. Then it sucks out blood with its mouth.

STRANGE NURSERY

A fish about the size of a small candy bar swims off the coast of Florida. It has large eyes, a big mouth, a yellow head, and a blue green body. It is called a yellowhead jawfish.

This fish lives near sandy reefs. It digs out a home on the seafloor and carries away the sand in its mouth. When the jawfish sees an enemy, it moves like lightning. It disappears down its hole, tail first. When it spots shrimp or another tasty meal, it dashes out and grabs it.

The yellowhead jawfish spends a lot of time near its home in the seafloor.

In spring, the female jawfish lays her eggs. She does not drop them in the sea, as many other fish do. Instead, she gives them to her mate to protect. The male jawfish carries them around in his mouth for about a week.

The male eats nothing until after the young hatch. But even after they are hatched, the young may rush back into a parent's mouth for safety. As they grow larger, however, their parents turn them away. The young soon become too big a mouthful.

The male yellowhead jawfish sometimes spits out the eggs and then sucks them back into his mouth. This helps the eggs get some air.

POISON

It's night and a hungry rattlesnake is moving through tall grass. It stops and flicks its forked tongue in and out of its mouth. The tip of its tongue passes over a special spot on the roof of its mouth. It is the snake's "smelling" organ. It helps the **reptile** know if food is nearby.

A rat is searching for seeds in the grass. The snake does not see the animal in the dark. But it smells it. It also senses body heat as the rat comes closer.

Rattlesnakes pick up scents by flicking their tongues in and out of their mouth.

The snake opens its mouth wide. Two **fangs** appear. These hollow teeth have been folded against the roof of the snake's mouth. Now they swing out and pierce the rat's body.

The snake's muscles squeeze **venom** through the fangs. The poison enters the rat's body. In minutes, the animal stops breathing. Slowly the snake begins swallowing the lifeless body headfirst. Once again, its poison-filled mouth has helped the snake find and capture food.

This rattlesnake shows two sharp fangs. The fangs release venom into the snake's prey.

MORE MOUTHPARTS

Large groups of prairie dogs live together in underground homes. They are careful not to let strangers enter. Everyone sits up straight when other prairie dogs come near. They touch the newcomers' lips to make certain no strangers are in the group.

Prairie dogs get to know one another by touching lips.

Birds don't have lips, but they do have differently shaped **bills**. And these bills can do more than kiss. They can clean feathers, crack seeds, build nests, and turn eggs. Some bills can even catch and kill prey.

The long, pointed bills of herons can catch and spear fish and snakes.

The fat bills of oystercatchers hammer and open oyster shells. The large bills of pelicans catch and carry fish. The hooked beaks of hawks and falcons tear the flesh of prey into bite-size pieces.

The beaks of ospreys are curved and pointed to help them tear apart prey.

Tongues of birds and other creatures are also handy tools. The woodpecker's tongue can reach deep inside tree holes to pull out hidden insects. The chameleon's tongue is even longer and can snatch prey out of the air.

A chameleon's tongue is extremely long. It is fast enough to catch insects in midair.

But the prize for the longest tongue goes to the giant anteater. It can reach a meal 2 feet (0.6 meter) away. It flicks its tongue in and out of its mouth about 150 times a minute. Each time it does, ants get stuck on sticky saliva on the tongue. The giant anteater's tongue catches about 30,000 insects a day.

A giant anteater sticks out its long pink tongue to catch insects from a bush.